HOW I BECAME A PSYCHOLOGIST

HOW I BECAME A PSYCHOLOGIST

poems

Henry M. Seiden

Copyright © 2017 by Henry M. Seiden

International Psychoanalytic Books (IPBooks),
30-27 33rd Street, #3R
Astoria, NY 11102
Online at: www.IPBooks.net

All rights reserved. No part of this book may be used or reproduced in any manner whatsoever including Internet usage, without written permission of the author.

Cover photograph by Edith W. Seiden, cover design by Josh Seiden.
Interior book design by Maureen Cutajar, gopublished.com

ISBN: 978-0-9995965-2-4

for Sara

*and with thanks to Gail Mazur, Rosalind Pace, my Truro poets' group,
my old Bronx friends, my loving family and all the teachers
I've encountered on the road....*

Table of Contents

	INTRODUCTION	ix
1.	GRANDMOTHERS	1
2.	SNEEZE	2
3.	ICE CREAM CONES	3
4.	YANKEE STADIUM	4
5.	TEACHERS	5
6.	BETRAYAL	6
7.	SHAKESPEARE	7
8.	SOCIOLOGY	8
9.	OLD FORGE, NY	9
10.	CANOE	12
11.	MISS BRODIE	13
12.	SOCRATES	14
13.	FRENCH	15
14.	POOL HALL	16
15.	PSYCHOLOGY	18
16.	UNION	19
17.	HAIRCUT	20
18.	ISAAC BASHEVIS SINGER AND MARY HENLE	21
19.	HOWE, FAULKNER AND MACK	22
20.	DUGAN	23
21.	RORSCHACH	24
22.	RECURRING DREAM	25

Introduction

These poems, which can be read as a kind of autobiography, recall deepening moments of perplexity, question, and discovery—those peculiar or unsettling or disturbing or surprising or funny or valuable lessons that one learns, like it or not, growing up. I think that an *almost-knowing, never to be full....* (which I call it in one of these poems) is at the intellectual center of what has become my life's work. If anything, it's a pleasurable uncertainty that grows stronger—in all I do as a poet and all I do as a psychoanalytic psychotherapist.

HMS
September 2017

1. Grandmothers

My sweet grandmother would look at me sadly sometimes
—as she watched me eat her sugar cookies
at the kitchen table. *Henry,* she'd say, *nothing stays the same....*

I know, Grandma, I'd say – only because I loved her.

My other grandmother told me that some nights
she cried for her own mother.

They talked to me—if never to each other.

My mother told me that death was *just like sleeping,*
which even then I didn't believe, and that, *not-to-worry,*
it doesn't happen until you get much older.

Aren't old people afraid of dying? I asked her.
By that time, she said, *they get used to the idea.*

2. Sneeze

Gezuntheit! Grandma said, when I sneezed.
And sometimes: *You sneeze on the truth!*

But Grandma, I'd say, *I have allergies!*
We'd both laugh—at the idea

that there could be so many truths;
and at what a *wisenheimer* I was already.

But I knew that she wasn't only-laughing.
She kept a picture by her bedside

of her baby, Saul, who died of diphtheria.
A cold is not a thing to sneeze at.

3. Ice Cream Cones
1946

My little sister and I each had a dime,
from our Uncle Lou, the same who
liked to give us the bands from his cigars
to wear as rings. We were off to *Addie Vallins*
for ice cream cones.

My father (being sensible), took my dime
and hers and paid for all three
(that is, including his) with a dollar bill.

We were licking our cones and walking home
when Rita said she wanted *her* dime back.
*Daddy bought them with his dollar bill;
her dime was still in his pocket.* She insisted.

He tried to explain. I was at the age of reason,
at least *an* age of reason, and tried to explain too.
She became more & more upset.

Now here's the tough part: he gave her back *her* dime—
and didn't give me mine. I knew he did it because
she was cute. At least he thought so.

4. *Yankee Stadium*
Bronx, late 40s

Beyond the park, a few blocks down,
always there, looming large: the Stadium
where the big game would be going on—
unfolding but unseen. When they played at night,
the sky was lit by the glow of lights. But
day or night, you heard a consequential hum,
sometimes a roar, rising with a hit? signaling
a run? or ending abruptly—a disappointing foul?
We could almost tell. Like all of childhood,
it was an almost-knowing, never to be full.
Who did what? and how? Was this the sound
of good news? or of bad? We'd stop
our own street game to ask a passing fan,
usually a guy with his tie undone, a scorecard
in his hand: *Hey Mister!* we'd call, *Who won?*

5. *Teachers*

My great-grandfather, *the Great Zeyde*,
they called him, was a *rebbe*.
We saw his photograph, the white beard
spreading across his chest; we heard about
his lessons—the form his corrections took:
a thimble on his forefinger the better
to ping some reluctant scholar
like my uncle or my father on the top
of his *dempfool* head. Despite which
or maybe because of it, my father
became a teacher, high school math,
like my uncle, a teacher like my mother & my aunt,
(even a cousin, even my mother's mother
—even their socialist friends). When there was
visiting, there would be tests: arithmetic,
geography, how do you spell spaghetti?
I read out loud from the *Times* when I was so small
I had to lie on my belly on the Persian rug.
There was applause & laughter but it was never
about curiosity. They asked lots of *whats*.
They left to the kids to ask the *whys*.

6. Betrayal
age ten

Danny L. was the ninth of ten kids
of the Irish family who lived upstairs on 6.
I was a bookish kid who read *Tom Sawyer*
every chance I got. Hanging out with Danny
I could get a little taste of a Tom Sawyer life.

Danny's school was parochial; his way
was to be in trouble, I'm not sure I ever thought
there was any hidden good in him. (Although
I'm sure someone would have found something nice
to say about him at his funeral).

If there was a fight, he was in it, if there was
an argument, you'd want to be on his side of it.
I admired his toughness, but was always scared of him a little.
He liked me—only now I see it—for the stories I dreamed up
(which maybe was his hidden good).

I told tales – from the books I read
or of libidinal adventures I swore I'd had.
After one long afternoon of invention & fantasy,
he had to leave to get home before his father did.
(His *Pop* was the one thing he lived in fear of.)
At the door, he called my tales *a pack of lies.*

7. Shakespeare

My mother loved Shakespeare, my father
and me and my little sister but not always in that order
—her grandchildren too, to be fair.

But she *lived* for Shakespeare.
Which, I know, is not the same as loving.
Her Shakespeare group met in our apartment in the Bronx.
I got to read bit parts—a sailor in *The Tempest*.

My friend Bromberg says it's impossible
for anyone to be "fair" to his mother,
that there are a million explanations as to why—
but, in all fairness, no one better than the next.

8. Sociology

We stop at the *Court* deli for a hotdog,
a cup of tea, a soda, nothing pricey.
The waiter tosses our food onto the table.
Even at eleven I can see he's rude.
Still my father leaves a tip—maybe a dime.
When we go out, I ask him why?
Look, my father says, *He wasn't meant to be a waiter!*
No Jewish boy was ever meant to be a waiter....

My father's lessons had a way of being hard
to get a grip on. The etiquette of the delicatessen?
Embarrassment at being taken for a piker?
A kind of I-grew-up-here sociology?
A there-but-for-the grace sympathy?
We were going to play tennis in Mullaly Park;
while that poor *schmuck* was stuck—in the deli
by the court house on 161st Street in the Bronx.

9. *Old Forge, NY*
early 1950s summer vacations

Bears
Horace Wallace, a hunter when he had the chance,
had a hi-beam searchlight attached to the window
of his '49 Ford. He liked to drive out to the town dump,

taking his son Davey and me, to watch black bears
rummaging through the smoldering garbage. The beam
cut through the smokiness & haze of the Adirondack night.

The bears, like big, slow-moving but graceful dogs were
untroubled by the spotlight's intrusion. We were warned
to stay in the car. Although I myself had little taste

for getting any closer to the wildness. The bears were
un-hurried, almost casual. It was the way you might dream
of bears, bears at a distance—with more curiosity than alarm.

Rain
In that mountain village, there could be rain showers
so light you'd barely feel them—the raindrops
more like mist. And this when the sun was shining.

Sometimes, for a minute, it might rain on one side
of the street and not the other! We'd leave our bikes in a pile
on the sidewalk and walk out onto Main Street, palms up,

trying to find the place where you'd could feel the rain
on one hand and not feel it on the other.
I was 13—and on both sides of my own dividing line.

Ring
I lost my ring when I was 10 (a birthday present,
thin, gold, my initials on it)—over the side of my father's canoe.

I'd put it in my shoe to keep it safe. We were returning to the dock.
Forgetting, I knocked my shoe on the gunwale to empty out the sand & dirt.

Like that! The ring was gone! I watched it sink.
I stripped; I dove for it—again & again—hoping to catch a glint.

My father was patient—a patience unusual for him.
I knew he felt as helpless as I felt—but it was getting cold and late.

A lot of time has passed since then. My ring, I think, is down there still,
in Old Forge Pond—buried in the silt.

10. Canoe

I want to give my Dad his due: his red canoe, a summer day,
a picnic and a swim at a little island in Fourth Lake.

Of course, we swam "b.a." I was shy about my body
but he exulted in every opportunity to swim *au naturel*.

He insisted—to anyone who'd listen—that FDR
should have added this, fifth one, to his "four freedoms"—

a line which took him back to his own young manhood,
camping with his brother, Norman, on an island in Lake George.

That day we stayed out longer than we should have.
The sky was getting dark, the wind against us, picking up.

I was tired now and frightened. He said, *It's OK, Henry
lie down in the bottom of the boat—just go to sleep.*

I woke up at the dock.

11. Miss Brodie

Seventh Grade, Jordan L. Mott Junior High School,
(Don't ask me who Jordan L. Mott was; no one cared
or knew: let's just call it JHS 22.)

My English teacher Miss Brodie (and don't ask me
if she was in her prime—she looked pretty old to me—
maybe she was forty) taught "creative writing,"

an elective I signed up for. She smiled, pleased,
surprised by my choice. But it was not to be.
Walter persuaded me to switch to "social dance"

where I would learn the Lindy, and the Cha Cha
and get to dance with Ilona and Ruthie. I had to tell Miss B.
She was disappointed, maybe hurt. I could see that

in her face. And now the one surprised was me:
I didn't think this was a difference I could make.

12. Socrates

Bronx Science, Sophomore year, Geometry. Mr. B.
thought he was Socrates and that we were slaves
in the market place. *Mister—eh—Seiden,*

he'd say running his finger over his Delaney cards.
Up! On your feet, young man! Which I would do reluctantly
—bent a little at the waist & trying to hide a boner.

He himself was bent on framing a dialogue:
on the congruence of certain triangles,
on the shortest distance, on the height of *abc*....

I'd been thinking about Donna sitting next to me–
if you can call that thought. Who knows what Donna
was thinking. Non-Euclidian, I'd have to guess,
but, likely, not about me.

13. French

I saw my first French film at *The Astor*:
Fernadel, in *The Sheep Has Five Legs*, with Natalie
at the enlightened recommendation of our teacher
of 3rd Year French. *Bad guys in Tahiti on a ship
catch a fly and bet big money on whose cube of sugar
it will land on. It lights on & walks across a native woman's
naked breasts. It pauses de temps en temps
to rub its "hands"….* The subtitles become irrelevant;
the tension mounts. *Ou*, where, would things go next?

Much of what I thought about back then was breasts.
Maybe that was true for Natalie as well. We didn't
make out. We giggled. And we didn't talk about this.
We didn't know how. Not in English, not in French.

14. Pool Hall

Hookey players, the place always dark,
the air stale with b.o. & cigarette smoke.
One flight up. 161st Street in the Bronx.
We played "Chicago"—don't make me explain:
rotation, not straight pool, a nickel a "way";
lose seven, a roundhouse, that's fifty cents.

I thought I was good—played all summer
on a table in a basement somewhere else.
I was loose, running five six seven balls,
pocketing them *like they had eyes* (we used to say).
One of the wise guys, Singer, by name,
says: *Come on, Seiden, let's play for quarters.*
Table one! A quarter a way.

A hard hitter, Singer; he knew *ass beats class.*
Maybe you can guess what happened next?
Guys watching—bets on the side. My grip gets shaky:
I scratch—on the break! I lose big – and fast:
two fifty, first rack. Crapped out. Tapped.
Lucky for me, friends bail me out.

Truth is, it was Benny who rescued my ass.
He ran the place (and when he could)
protected us from hustles; judged disputes;
made sure there was no spitting and *no jump shots*
which tore the felt. Kept things cool
if it got raucous. (You'd applaud a good shot
by banging on the floor with the butt of your cue).

No hanging out down in the street. He said:
They'll call you 'fuckin bums from the pool hall.'
Bad enough you're fuckin bums—let's keep
the pool hall out of this.... Knew us all by name.
When the telephone rang, half the guys would yell,
Not here, Benny! Sometimes he taught technique.

Strategy too: *Chicago isn't straight pool....*
he liked point out. Position *helps, but, kid,*
just hit the low ball on the table. Hit it hard.
Whatever goes down, it's yours. In my case
that was the truth. Still, he couldn't save me—
notwithstanding the good advice: I wasn't meant for this.
Fat Singer was my denouement.

15. Psychology

Summer 1958, City College of New York.
I've failed out of Engineering, Freshman year,
(F in the physics of electricity; F in integral calc).
One, hard, way of telling myself what it was
I wasn't meant to be. Now to make it up—

Psych 1, in summer school. First day:
It's 8 o'clock & humid, the walls are a shade of green,
the windows are open in hope of catching a breeze.
Latecomers wander in; the group is half asleep.

Professor Resnikoff tells us a story:
A guy looks for a table in a cafeteria and sits down,
next to a good-looking woman in a seat that's free.
Soon he feels her leg against his knee! He gets so excited
he can't eat. As he's thinking what to say, she gets up
and leaves—leaving her "leg" in place!

Notwithstanding what he'd told himself he felt,
what he'd felt was a table leg. *This,* says Professor R,
his index finger raised, *is Psychology.*

I got an A.

16. Union

Freshman year, CCNY, Diana and I
got invited to a Union College *Homecoming*
by a friend. Maybe I should have known
Diana was already on to other things and "men,"

of which I wasn't one—but she wanted to go.
Something wasn't right: she was so sweet,
friendly all the way up the Hudson on the train,
when she'd always been a teasing kind of mean.

The campus was covered with snow.
My feet were cold and wet. The home team lost;
this wasn't *home* for us. Worse: She was *pretending*
to be giving: I could feel it when we touched.

Another growing-up, I guess: I came to know
that many times what looks like *yes* means *no*.

17. Haircut

Senior year, 1959. Sara wore her hair
in a *bohemian* braid—which spoke to me.
But her mother disagreed. To appease her,
Sara was willing to concede: She'd get the braid cut off.
On the phone she explained it in some agony.

I drove across the *Triboro* that Saturday night
rehearsing how I'd say: *Looks good to me....*
Instead, when she met me at the door, I said,
Oh, no.... She wailed. She ran inside;
she slammed her bedroom door.

The next week her mother (I give her credit),
took her to a better hairdresser to fix things up.
Again, Sara met me shyly at the door.
This time I said, *Wow, looks great!*
Let's get married! We laughed through tears.
Reader, she became my wife....

18. Isaac Bashevis Singer and Mary Henle

I heard Bashevis Singer read at the Y.

He said, *So ask me a question—if I can't answer it
I'll answer a different question.*

And he said,
I believe in free will—what choice do I have?
The audience loved him and that.

But as for answering the question: I got a D
from Mary Henle for my response to her question
on the Comprehensive Doctoral Qualifying Exam,
New School, 1968. And an A from Professor W—
who said *he* saw nothing wrong with the same answer.

The average was a failing grade. I had no choice
but to ask Professor Henle why (she of the grey cardigan,
whose reputation was: if you possibly can, stay away).
Oh! she said, *Yours would be a good answer—
to a different question.*

I had to admit she was right
even as I pleaded that I'd have to wait a year—
a year out of my young life—to take the Comps again.

She smiled her little smile. There was some compassion.
Next time, she said, *I'm sure you'll pass.*

19. Howe, Faulkner and Mack

At The New School, in the late sixties: *Time
& how we live it* was my topic. And in the course
of pursuing it I'd read an essay by Irving Howe
on time in Faulkner's *Sound and Fury*—

and then I met the man himself (Howe not Faulkner)
at a party given by his *then* wife, Professor Mack,
the *then* Chair of Psychology.

Howe had a drink in his hand. *Oh,* he said,
I remember that essay but I can't remember what I said....

He turned away. Which might have been the end.
But I stayed with *time* for my dissertation—which,
I have to say, at graduation won special mention.

20. Dugan

Sticks and Stones.... my mother said, *but words....*
But still, I can't forget a poetry workshop, Truro, Castle Hill,
1980, it would have been. The setting sweet: a tilted table
under the locust trees. A college kid (only a little
more pretentious than the rest of us); his poem,
with Muslim and Hindu references in a promiscuous mix.

Dugan, our teacher, takes a sip from his can of beer.
We wait. After a long silence, flat-voiced, he says:
There are parts of the world where you would be killed for this!
He doesn't say, *One of them is here.*

21. Rorschach

Kingsbrook Jewish Medical Center, internship:
1969, I'm administering the Rorschach to Mr. T,
a 69 year old white male....

What does he see? Nothing. He shrugs,
Maybe a bat, could be a butterfly....
Nothing & nothing doing.

I'm about to send him back to the Men's ward,
it's almost time for lunch, when a brown mouse creeps out
from behind the bookcase. Both of us sit up.

Ha! he says, *If there's one, there's thousands,
the walls are full of 'em....* He chuckles.
They'll own this fuckin place!

Still, he says, *I feel sorry for him.* Why's that?
...Once he shows himself, he's dead.

22. Recurring Dream

I'm in the ballpark, Yankee Stadium or
the Polo Grounds. I have a ticket
but my view's obscured.

I'm behind a pole in the Polo Grounds.
Or too high above the field, as when
the uptown IRT—just before

the 161st Street station—flashes past
the billboards behind the bleachers
& you get a glimpse of green.

Primal scene some would say, I know.
But questions abound: The Yankees?
The Giants (before they left New York)?

Giants, I suppose, makes some sense:
my parents getting something on
in the other room—and I'm not part of it.

Or there is some ceremony
I *have* been invited to but can't or won't
let myself see? What exclusion

is haunting me—what action is it
I'm not part of & never will be?

About the Author

Henry M. Seiden is a poet, psychologist and psychoanalyst who lives and practices in Forest Hills, New York.

His most recent books include: *Spaldeen: poems*, published by IP Books in 2016 and *The Motive for Metaphor: brief essays on poetry and psychoanalysis*, published by Karnac in 2016. He published *Tinnitus*, a chapbook of poems, in 2009.

He published *Grandpa White's Diary* (in 2013) and co-authored *Silent Grief: living in the wake of suicide* with Christpher Lukas (1986, Scribners) which continues in print with Jessica Kingsley.

He has poems in a number of literary journals and writes regularly on psychoanalytic subjects and on poetry.

www.ingramcontent.com/pod-product-compliance
Lightning Source LLC
Chambersburg PA
CBHW070553300426
44113CB00011B/1902